Hustling and Bustling
SUBMARINES

WHEELS AND AUTOMOBILES

FOX EYE
PUBLISHING

A submarine is a boat that travels beneath the surface of the water.

Deep under the sea there are wonderful things to see.

A submarine is awesome. It can dive
beneath the waves, into the deep below.

Down, down, down the submarine travels.
How far will it go?

surfer

Then, up and up the submarine moves, until it is above the waves. Next, a periscope pokes out, so submariners inside can see all about!

swimmer

sailor

A swimmer. A sailor. A surfer on the sea.
What else is in the picture? What can you see?

A submarine has an engine.
It gives it the power to move.

Some submarines have both an engine
and a battery too.

The submarine has ballast tanks. When the tanks fill with water, the submarine dives.

When the tanks fill with air,
it helps the submarine rise.

shark

The submarine is tough, made of metal through
and through. Its spinning propeller moves it along.
A shark whooshes past too!

propeller

Deep beneath the waves, it is as dark as night.
But inside the submarine are plenty of lights.

The submarine has mechanical arms.
It has a camera too.

Scientists study the ocean floor with special submarine tools.

shipwreck

The submarine is searching for treasures buried in the sand.

jewels

gold

It finds a shipwreck, with gold and jewels.
It must have once been grand!

whale

The submarine can tell when a whale is near.

Beeps tell it to go slow.
Away the submarine must steer.

school of fish

Past a school of fish the submarine glides.
A seahorse and a turtle watch the machine go by.

seahorse

turtle

At last, the submarine rises up again, towards the surface of the sea. Today's adventure is nearly over. What will tomorrow's be?

Bustling Words

A **ballast tank** is a container that can fill with water or air.

A **battery** is an object that makes electricity. Electricity is a type of power.

To **dive** means to go deeper underwater.

An **engine** is the part of a submarine that makes its energy.

Jewels are pretty stones, such as diamonds.

A **machine** is something that helps us to do work.

A **mechanical arm** is the arm of a machine.

Metal is a hard material that is used to make things.

A **periscope** is a special tool that sticks up above the water's surface to show what is there.

A **propeller** is a machine that makes a submarine move forwards.

A **shipwreck** is a ship that has sunk beneath the waves.

Steer means to make a vehicle go in a certain direction.

Submariners are people inside a submarine.

A **tool** is something that helps us to do a job. A hammer is a type of tool.

First published in 2024 by Fox Eye Publishing
Unit 31, Vulcan House Business Centre,
Vulcan Road, Leicester, LE5 3EF
www.foxeyepublishing.com

Author: Katherine Eason
Art director: Paul Phillips
Cover designer: Emma Bailey
Editor: Jenny Rush

All illustrations by Eszter Szepvolgyi

978-1-80445-343-8

Printed in China